D0845598

COOKING
AROUND THE WORLD

An Indian Cookbook for Kids

Rosemary Hankin

PowerKiDS
press

New York

Published in 2014 by The Rosen Publishing Group
29 East 21st Street, New York, NY 10010

Produced for Rosen by Calcium Creative Ltd
Editor for Calcium Creative Ltd: Sarah Eason
US Editor: Sara Howell
Designer: Paul Myerscough

Picture credits: Cover: Shutterstock: Privilege. Inside: Dreamstime: Mohammed Anwarul Kabir Choudhury 8tr, 8br, Beat Germann 17t, Gauravmasand 17b, Merzzie 25b, Luciano Mortula 13t, Olegd 5, Outline205 13b, Pipa100 7l, Paul Prescott 25t, Rcmathiraj 4br, Hara Sahani 4tr, Rechitan Sorin 21b, Yurchyk 7r, Zatletic 9; Shutterstock: Marilo Bertomeu 21, Chris Christou 18, Mukesh Kumar 14, Richard M Lee 22, Mageon 26, Silentwings 10, Wavebreakmedia 6; Tudor Photography: 11, 15, 19, 23, 27.

Library of Congress Cataloging-in-Publication Data

Hankin, Rosemary.
 An Indian cookbook for kids / by Rosemary Hankin.
    p. cm. — (Cooking around the world)
 Includes index.
 ISBN 978-1-4777-1338-9 (library binding) — ISBN 978-1-4777-1524-6 (pbk.) — ISBN 978-1-4777-1525-3 (6-pack)
 1. Cooking, Indic—Juvenile literature. 2. India—Social life and customs—Juvenile literature. I. Title.
 TX724.5.I4H26 2014
 641.5954—dc23
                                      2013003446

Manufactured in the United States of America

CPSIA Compliance Information: Batch #S13PK8: For Further Information contact Rosen Publishing, New York, New York at 1-800-237-9932

Contents

Delicious India

India is part of the continent of Asia. Enormous mountains called the Himalayas are in the north of India. They are the highest **mountain range** in the world. The huge Ganges River, which is 1,557 miles (2,505 km) long, begins in the Himalayas. India also has **desert** and **tropical forests**.

The national animal of India is the Bengal Tiger and the national flower is the lotus flower. There is even a modern **temple** in New Delhi called the Lotus Temple.

Indians think food is very important and the country even has a national fruit, the mango. People from different religions eat different food in India. Many people in India are **Hindus** or **Muslims**. Hindus do not eat beef and Muslims do not eat pork, for example. Many Indians do not eat meat at all. Most dishes are freshly made using vegetables, herbs, and lots of **spices**. Rice and bread are served at most meals.

The Lotus Temple in New Delhi is shaped like a lotus.

The Ganges River is important to Hindus. There are sacred sites on the river's banks.

Delicious curries are one of the most popular of Indian foods.

Get Set to Cook

Cooking is fun! There is nothing better than making food and then sharing it with your family and friends.

Every recipe page in this book starts with a "You Will Need" list. This is a set of **ingredients**. Be sure to collect everything on the list before you start cooking.

Look out for the "Top Tips" boxes. These have great tips to help you cook.

"Be Safe!" boxes warn you when you need to be extra careful.

Use one cutting board for meat and fish and a different cutting board for vegetables and fruit.

Always ask a grown-up if you can do some cooking.

Watch out for sharp knives! Ask a grown-up to help you with chopping and slicing.

Be sure to wash your hands before you start cooking.

Always wash any fruit and vegetables before using them.

Always ask a grown-up for help when cooking on the stove or using the oven.

Wear an apron to keep your clothes clean as you cook.

West Bengal

The area of West Bengal is found at the top of the Bay of Bengal. West Bengal is on the border with Bangladesh and its capital city is Calcutta. It lies on the banks of the Hugli River and was once the capital of India when the British ruled the country.

Bengali Cooking

Bengalis eat a lot of rice, lentils, fish, and vegetables. Sometimes they wrap fish in pumpkin leaves to cook them. They use coconut in their dishes, and lots of spices to bring out the flavor of their food. Some dishes are mild and some are quite spicy.

Sweet Treats

Sweets and desserts, called *mishti*, are popular in Bengal. Bengalis make delcious sweets using cottage cheese. These include *chanar payesh*, which is made with pistachio nuts and cardamom spice. Bengalis love *sandesh*, which is a dish that is served at the end of a meal. It is a little like a milk jelly and is flavored with almonds and saffron.

Fish wrapped in pumpkin leaves is one of the tasty dishes eaten in West Bengal.

Street vendors make fresh juices to order. So delicious!

Sweetmeats are balls of sugar and milk that are fried. They are a popular dessert.

Aloo Ka Paratha

YOU WILL NEED:

5 medium-size potatoes,
    peeled, boiled, and mashed
2 tsp ground coriander
1 tsp ground cumin
½ tsp cumin seeds
½ tsp ground turmeric
1 tsp chili powder
salt, to taste
3 tbsp fresh cilantro,
    finely chopped
2 inch (5 cm) piece fresh
    ginger root, finely grated
2 cups all-purpose flour
2 tbsp vegetable oil
water, to mix

These tasty flatbreads are stuffed with mashed potatoes and **seasoned** with spices and other flavorings. *Parathas* are eaten for breakfast in India, with chutneys and pickles. You can also eat them with yogurt.

BE SAFE!
• Ask a grown-up to help you prepare the potatoes.
• Watch out for your fingers when you are grating the fresh ginger root.

STEP 1

In a bowl, mix the mashed potatoes with the spices, salt, cilantro, and ginger. Set aside.

STEP 2

Put the flour and vegetable oil in a mixing bowl. Rub together until the mixture is crumbly. Add water, a little at a time. Knead well to make a dough. Cover with a clean dishtowel and set aside for 1 hour.

STEP 3

Divide the dough into pieces about the size of golf balls. Flatten the balls into circles. Then spoon some potato mixture into the centers. Fold the edges of the circles in over the potato and pat to flatten.

STEP 4

Heat a griddle pan and cook the parathas. Place in the pan and flip when you start to see bubbles. Oil the paratha then flip again. Oil the other side and flip. Continue until crisp and golden on both sides.

TOP TIP You could use whole wheat flour, if you prefer, for your parathas.

Punjabi Tastes

The **state** of Punjab is in the northwest of India. Its name means "Land of Five Waters" because the state has five rivers. A lot of farming takes place in Punjab because the soil there is so rich and the supply of river water makes it easy to water crops.

Punjabi Food

Punjabis like rich food. Milk, butter, and cream are used in most dishes. Both wheat and corn are grown in Punjab and made into lots of different kinds of bread. Tandoori roti, naan, parathas, and *kulcha* are all popular, especially stuffed parathas. In Punjab, people eat rice only at very special meals, such as wedding or birthday celebration meals.

Spicy Mixtures

Punjabi cooks use a lot of onion, garlic, fresh ginger, and tomatoes in their cooking. They also like to use spices. This is why so many of their dishes are called "masala," which means "a spicy mixture." Spices used include coriander seeds, cumin, and cloves. Punjabi people also cook with black pepper, red chili, and mustard. These spices make the food taste very hot. Turmeric is used to add an earthy flavor and a lovely yellow color to dishes.

The Golden Temple at Amritsar is one of the most famous places in Punjab.

Street vendors cook and sell tasty breads on the sidewalks and in the markets of Punjab cities.

Rajma

YOU WILL need:

2 tbsp sunflower oil
1 tsp cumin seeds
2 onions, finely chopped
2 inch (5 cm) piece fresh
    ginger root
6 garlic cloves, crushed
2 large tomatoes, chopped
    into 1 inch (2.5 cm) cubes
2 fresh green chilies,
    finely chopped
2 tsp ground coriander
1 tsp ground cumin
¼ tsp ground turmeric
1 tsp garam masala
2 x 15 ounce (425 g)
    cans kidney beans
salt, to taste

This vegetarian curry is a favorite in Punjabi cooking. Kidney beans are cooked with onions, tomatoes, and spices. *Rajma* goes well with boiled rice and is a great, spicy dish to try on a cold, wintry day.

BE SAFE!
- Be careful when opening the cans.
- Ask a grown-up to help with the chopping.

STEP 1

Heat the oil in a pan and add the cumin seeds. When they start sizzling, add the onion and **sauté**. Add the ginger and garlic and sauté for 2 minutes.

STEP 2

Now add the green chilies, tomatoes, ground coriander, cumin, turmeric, and garam masala. Then sauté, stirring, until the oil separates from the mixture.

STEP 3

Drain and rinse the kidney beans. Add to the pan with 3 cups warm water and add salt to taste. Cook until the beans are very soft, around 10 minutes. Mash the beans slightly to thicken the sauce.

STEP 4

Serve the rajma hot with rice and perhaps a cucumber salad and your favorite pickled vegetable.

TOP TIP Cook this dish the day before you want to eat it. Leave it overnight and it will taste even better!

Beautiful Kerala

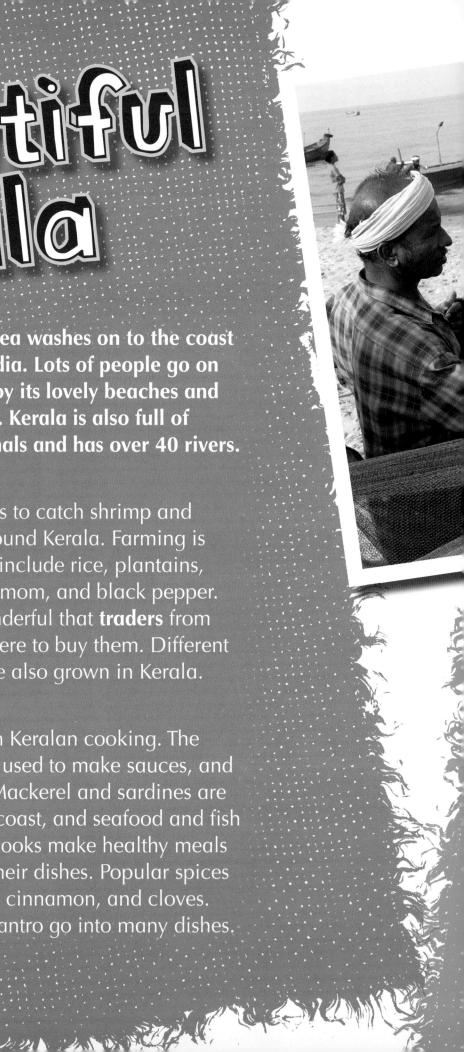

The beautiful Arabian Sea washes on to the coast of Kerala in southwest India. Lots of people go on vacation to Kerala to enjoy its lovely beaches and the warm, sunny weather. Kerala is also full of beautiful plants and animals and has over 40 rivers.

Fishing and Farming

Fishermen use large nets to catch shrimp and fish in the shallow sea around Kerala. Farming is also important and crops include rice, plantains, coconuts, cashews, cardamom, and black pepper. Keralan spices are so wonderful that **traders** from all over the world come here to buy them. Different types of tea and coffee are also grown in Kerala.

Cooking in Kerala

Coconut is often used in Keralan cooking. The flesh is grated, the milk is used to make sauces, and coconut oil is used, too. Mackerel and sardines are cooked every day on the coast, and seafood and fish are often eaten. Keralan cooks make healthy meals and use lots of spices in their dishes. Popular spices include cumin, coriander, cinnamon, and cloves. Fresh curry leaves and cilantro go into many dishes.

Fishermen pull their nets on to the beach. They will mend them before they go out for another catch.

Locally-caught fish are used to make delicious Keralan dishes.

Lassi

YOU WILL need:

1/8 tsp saffron threads

1 x 15 ounce (425 g) can sliced mango/mango pulp or 1 large fresh mango

2 cups plain yogurt

2/3 cup milk or unsweetened condensed milk

1/4 cup superfine sugar

2 cups crushed ice

This is a yogurt-based Indian drink. It can be **savory** or sweet. On a very hot day, lassi is a great way to **quench** your thirst. Sweet varieties use many different fruits.

BE SAFE!

• If you are using canned mango, be careful when opening the can.

• Ask a grown-up to operate the blender.

STEP 1

Using a pestle and mortar, grind the saffron threads until they turn into a powder. Pour in around half the milk or condensed milk and stir until well combined.

STEP 2

If you are using a fresh mango, ask a grown-up to halve it and then make crosswise and lengthwise cuts on the mango halves. Press on the skin side so the halves look like little orange porcupines!

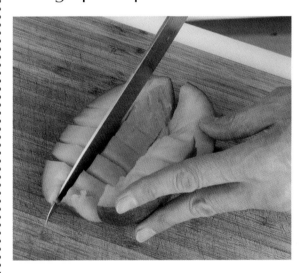

TOP TIP   If the mixture in the blender is too stiff, add a little water.

STEP 3

Peel off the squares of mango with your fingers or use a small, sharp knife. Then carefully cut the remaining flesh from around the **pit**.

STEP 4

Put the mango pieces or pulp, plain yogurt, the remaining milk or condensed milk, sugar, crushed ice, and the ground saffron mixture in a blender.

STEP 5

Blend for about 2 minutes. The mixture should become smooth and creamy. Pour into tall glasses to serve.

Rich Rajasthan

The state of Rajasthan is in the northwest of India, next to Pakistan. It is hilly in the southeast and a desert called the Thar Desert is in the northwest. Many different **tribes** live in Rajasthan. Some of them wear bright clothes and lots of jewelry.

Taste of Rajasthan

Rajasthanis cook using ghee. This is butter that has been boiled. It can sometimes be hard to find water in Rajasthan, so people often use milk instead of water to cook. Rajasthanis do not cook many fresh green vegetables because it is hard to grow plants in this part of India. Instead, they eat lentils and beans. They also love sweet dishes, which are served before the main course.

Spicy Chutney

A chutney is a sauce made of pickled fruits and spices. Pickled foods, such as fruits and vegetables, are preserved in vinegar or brine. Chutneys are flavored with spices and sugar. Rajasthani chutneys use turmeric, coriander seed, mint, and garlic.

Rajasthani markets have lots of lentils and beans for sale.

Colorful cooking spices are sold in Rajasthani markets.

Chicken Biryani

This dish is often served on special occasions. The raisins in it give the chicken a sweet taste. The dish also contains whole spices. Don't eat them, though! They are used just to give the food a tasty flavor.

YOU WILL NEED:

1½ cups basmati rice
2 tbsp butter
1 large onion, finely sliced
1 bay leaf
3 cardamom pods
1 small cinnamon stick
1 tsp ground turmeric
4 skinless, boneless chicken breast fillets, cubed
4 tbsp curry paste
1¼ cups raisins
3½ cups chicken stock
scallions, finely sliced, to **garnish**

BE SAFE!
• Use separate cutting boards for vegetables and meat.
• Ask a grown-up to slice the onion.

STEP 1

Place the rice in a large strainer and rinse under cold running water until the water runs clear. Set aside.

STEP 2

Heat the butter in a large pan. Cook the onions with the bay leaf, cardamom pods, and cinnamon stick for 10 minutes, stirring occasionally. Stir in the turmeric. Add the chicken and curry paste. Cook until the chicken is no longer pink and the juices run clear.

STEP 3

Stir the rice into the pan. Add the raisins and pour in the stock. Cover the pan with a lid and bring to a hard boil. Lower the heat and cook for 10 minutes. Now turn off the heat and leave for 10 minutes more.

STEP 4

Garnish with the scallions and then serve while hot.

TOP TIP You can buy prepared curry paste in many grocery stores.

23

Delhi Delights

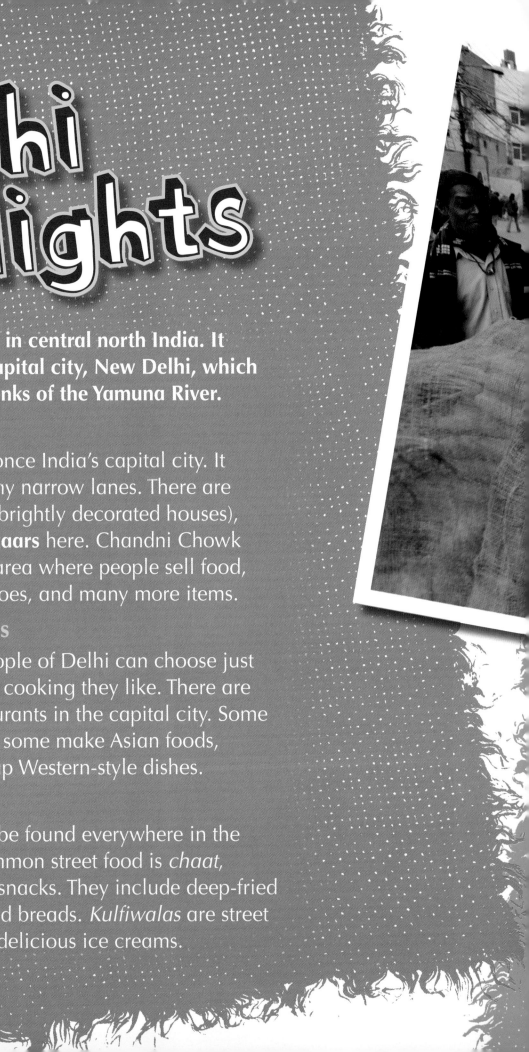

Delhi is an area in central north India. It includes India's capital city, New Delhi, which is found on the banks of the Yamuna River.

Old Delhi

Old Delhi was once India's capital city. It is made up of many narrow lanes. There are lots of old *haveli* (brightly decorated houses), **mosques**, and **bazaars** here. Chandni Chowk is a huge market area where people sell food, spices, clothes, shoes, and many more items.

Fantastic Flavors

The wealthy people of Delhi can choose just about any style of cooking they like. There are hundreds of restaurants in the capital city. Some cook Indian food, some make Asian foods, and others serve up Western-style dishes.

Street Food

Food stalls can be found everywhere in the city. The most common street food is *chaat*, which are savory snacks. They include deep-fried pastries and stuffed breads. *Kulfiwalas* are street sellers who serve delicious ice creams.

Street food and street markets are found all over Delhi. These street vendors are selling fresh vegetables.

City sidewalks are filled with spicy snacks for sale.

Sesame Cookies

YOU WILL NEED:

4 cups all-purpose flour
pinch of salt
¼ tsp baking soda
1 cup superfine sugar
1 stick (½ cup) butter, at
    room temperature, diced
3 eggs
1 tbsp caraway seeds
½ cup sesame seeds
½ cup milk

These little cookies are simple and fun to make. They are a healthy option, too! The sesame and caraway seeds give the cookies a lovely, nutty flavor. They taste delicious as both an after-meal treat or as a sweet snack.

BE SAFE!
- Ask a grown-up to help you use the oven.
- Always use oven mitts.

STEP 1

Preheat the oven to 350°F (180°F). Grease a baking sheet. Sift the flour with the salt and baking soda into a mixing bowl. Add the sugar, butter, 2 eggs, and the caraway seeds, then mix the ingredients.

STEP 2

Stir in the milk a little at a time. Then knead the mixture with your hands to form a smooth dough. Gather the dough into a ball. Sprinkle the work surface with flour. Roll out the dough to just under 1 inch (2.5 cm) thick.

STEP 3

Cut out the cookies using a cookie cutter. Beat the remaining egg and brush it over the cookies. Sprinkle the sesame seeds on the top, coating each cookie well.

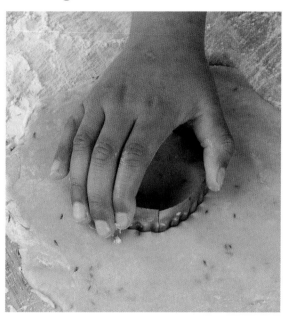

STEP 4

Place the cookies on the prepared baking sheet. Bake them in the preheated oven for around 10 minutes.

TOP TIP Use differently shaped cookie cutters if you wish. Reduce the baking time for thin cookie shapes.

Indian Meals on the Map!

Punjab

NEW DELHI

Rajasthan

India

Chicken Biryani

Lassi

Kerala

Now that you have discovered how to cook the delicious foods of India, find out where they are cooked and eaten on this map of the country.

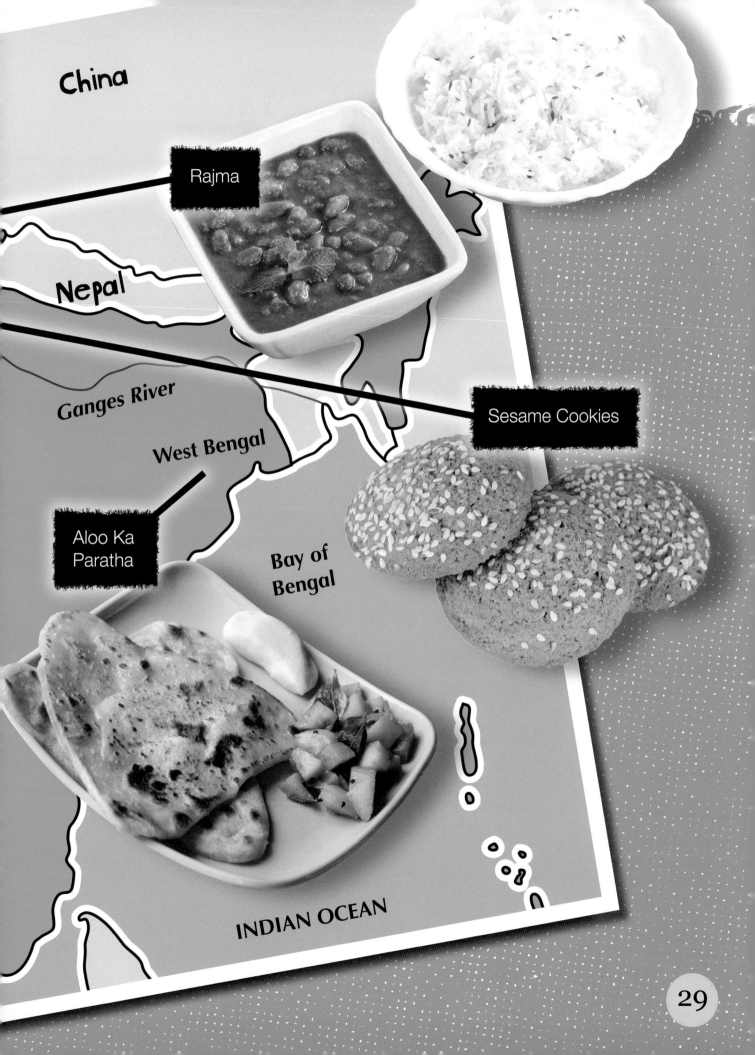

China

Rajma

Nepal

Ganges River

West Bengal

Aloo Ka
Paratha

Sesame Cookies

Bay of
Bengal

INDIAN OCEAN

Glossary

bazaars (buh-ZARZ) Indoor markets.

desert (DEH-zurt) An area that has almost no rain and so has very few plants.

garnish (GAR-nish) To decorate food before serving.

Hindus (HIN-dooz) People who believe in Hinduism, a faith in India.

ingredients (in-GREE-dee-untz) Different foods and seasonings that are used to make a recipe.

mosques (MOSKS) Muslim places of worship.

mountain range (MOWN-tun RAYNJ) An area that has many mountains.

Muslims (MUZ-lumz) People who practice the Islamic faith.

pit (PIHT) The hard center in the middle of some fruit.

quench (KWENCH) To stop being thirsty.

sauté (saw-TAY) To lightly fry food in oil or butter.

savory (SAY-vuh-ree) Food that is not sweet in taste.

seasoned (SEE-zun-ed) Given flavor.

spices (SPYS-ez) Powders that are rich in taste and which are used to add flavor to food.

state (STAYT) An area of a country that may have its own laws.

temple (TEM-pel) A place where people go to worship.

traders (TRAY-derz) People who buy and sell goods.

tribes (TRYBZ) Groups of people who live together and who have the same beliefs and ways of doing things.

tropical forests (TRAH-puh-kul FOR-ests) Forests with a very high rainfall.

Further Reading

Atkinson, Tim. *Discover India*. Discover Countries. New York: PowerKids Press, 2012.

Ganeri, Anita. *India*. A World of Food. Minneapolis, MN: Clara House Books, 2010.

Goodman, Polly. *Food in India*. Food Around the World. New York: PowerKids Press, 2008.

Websites

Due to the changing nature of Internet links, PowerKids Press has developed an online list of websites related to the subject of this book. This site is updated regularly. Please use this link to access the list:
www.powerkidslinks.com/caw/indi

Index